HAND to PAW

Protecting
Animals

Jessica Cohn

Consultants

Timothy Rasinski, Ph.D.
Kent State University

Lori Oczkus
Literacy Consultant

Thorsten Pape
Animal Trainer and Behaviorist

Based on writing from
TIME For Kids. TIME For Kids and the *TIME For Kids* logo are registered trademarks of TIME Inc. Used under license.

Publishing Credit

Dona Herweck Rice, *Editor-in-Chief*
Lee Aucoin, *Creative Director*
Jamey Acosta, *Senior Editor*
Lexa Hoang, *Designer*
Stephanie Reid, *Photo Editor*
Rane Anderson, *Contributing Author*
Rachelle Cracchiolo, *M.S.Ed., Publisher*

Teacher Created Materials
5301 Oceanus Drive
Huntington Beach, CA 92649-1030
http://www.tcmpub.com
ISBN 978-1-4333-4867-9
© 2013 Teacher Created Materials, Inc.

Table of Contents

Celebrate Animals

Animals live everywhere on Earth. Insects, mammals, reptiles, birds, and fish come in every color and shape you can imagine. They hunt, mate, and build their homes around the world.

Wild animals have fascinated people for thousands of years. Their strength and beauty have inspired and awed us. Their meat has served as food. Their furs have kept us warm. Animal bones were even used to make some of the first human tools.

Domesticated animals live on farms. They help with herding sheep, producing milk, and making **fertilizer**. Domesticated animals can also be our pets. Cats, dogs, iguanas, and even mice can be pets. The animals we bring into our homes can comfort and care for us. And we care for them.

Wild and domestic animals all play a role in our world. Humans are animals, too. But unlike most animals, we have power to think and make choices. We can protect and care for other animals.

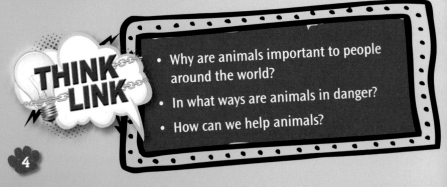

THINK LINK

- Why are animals important to people around the world?
- In what ways are animals in danger?
- How can we help animals?

Animals can be our best friends or ferocious predators, but they all need our protection.

In the Wild

Earth's animals come in a wild assortment. You know the long-necked giraffe and the harsh spikes of the porcupine. But there are many other strange creatures we are just discovering. In Africa, there is a spider that makes a web stronger than a bulletproof vest! In the Gulf of Mexico, **biologists** found an odd fish that walks on its fins. Scientists are calling it the pancake batfish.

Energy flows throughout the ecosystem in the form of food.

Each wild animal plays a big role in our **environment**. Larger animals eat smaller ones. Some animals eat plants. This helps to spread seeds. All the animals in an **ecosystem** are connected. Adding or removing just one animal can destroy the balance.

Even the smallest animals are important.

Larger predators gain energy from the ecosystem in many ways.

Fast Facts

Scientists discover new **species** every week. And they estimate there are still millions of animals to discover. Check out some of the most extreme animals found so far.

Extremely Fast

The cheetah is the fastest animal on land. In the heat of the hunt, it can run up to 68 miles per hour. That's the same speed as a car on the freeway!

Extremely Big

As far as we know, the blue whale is the largest animal that has ever lived. It can weigh over 150 tons, which is about as much as a locomotive.

WOW

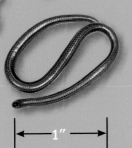

Extremely Weird

The leafy sea dragon is a relative of the sea horse. It lives in the southern waters of Australia. It is hard to see because it looks like floating seaweed.

Extremely Small

The smallest snake in the world is found on the island of Barbados. It is as thin as spaghetti. And it is only about four inches long.

|← 1″ →|

Extremely Colorful

Peacocks have beautifully colored iridescent-blue tail feathers. They show them off to win over females.

Animal IQ

Scientists want to know if animals think like us. They study how animals communicate with one another. They try to learn whether animals have emotions. Many people wonder how intelligent animals are. To find out, scientists watch what animals do. Many animals have special calls. They warn of danger from predators. Animals that hear these calls know to be alert. Some people say this shows they use language in ways similar to humans. Some animals can also make facial **expressions**. Dogs snarl and bare their teeth. This warns that they are angry. Baby chimps look and sound like human babies. Their cuteness attracts help in the same way. Chimps scream to tell others they are angry. They also use **gestures** to communicate. Some chimps have even learned human sign language.

chimpanzee

red-winged blackbird

Big Hearts

Scientists have found that whales may have similar emotions to humans. Whales have been observed putting themselves in harm's way to help others. They sometimes stay close to a dying whale.

Big Brains

Elephants, like humans, learn from their parents. They are taught how to eat. They learn how to use tools. Young ones learn how to live in the elephant community. Elephants can be problem solvers. One elephant in **captivity** removed the hook that was holding his chains. Then he helped the other elephants remove theirs.

Companions

Anyone who has a pet knows exactly how smart and caring animals can be. More than half of American homes have **companion** animals. Animals can be great friends. Children learn responsibility when they take care of them. People with pets are often calmer. They enjoy better health. Dog owners get exercise when they walk their dogs. Those who live alone feel needed when they give a home to a pet. Living with animals helps people get along better with other people, too.

Many cats and dogs live in shelters. They are waiting for someone to take them home. If you help an animal, you help yourself. You can live a longer, happier life.

Top 10 Pets

What are the top pets in America? These are recent rankings. Each year, the numbers change a bit.

1 dogs

2 cats

3 birds

4 fish

5 horses

Special Care

Some people say there is no such thing as an animal owner. Rather, a person is an animal guardian. This difference is a reminder that animals are not just objects. Animals have needs of their own.

People have kept dogs as pets for over 14,000 years.

6 rabbits

7 hamsters

9 turtles

8 guinea pigs

10 gerbils

13

Animals do more than simply comfort us. They can be trained to help people live and work. Dogs are popular **service animals**. Every year, hundreds are trained to help the blind. They help people stay safe and find their way in new places. Monkeys, pigs, and small horses have been trained as service animals. Parrots and goats have even been used, too. These animals can pick up objects that are hard to reach. Or, they can help care for someone who is injured. Other animals are used in hospitals to cheer up sick and lonely patients.

There is also a wide range of **working animals**. These animals do tasks that are difficult for people to do. Some dogs herd sheep. Others are search-and-rescue dogs. Police use scent-tracking dogs to find people. Horses and mules can pull carts. The military uses dolphins and sea lions to search in the water. Pigeons have been trained to carry messages over 500 miles. In many ways, animals make our lives easier.

Dolphins train with the military.

Mules are used to harvest wheat.

Puppy Love

You can help train a service animal. Puppies are placed in homes so they can learn how to behave at a very young age. When they are trained to obey orders, they are moved to a new home. There, they learn more advanced skills. You can **volunteer** to care for one of these dogs. You'll need to give the dog away when it is trained. But you will know it is going to a home where it will be loved and appreciated.

Creature Concerns

Animals amaze and inspire us. But they face many challenges. Some animals have been raised over time to live with people. Dogs and sheep were some of the first animals to be domesticated. They depend on people. They need us to provide food and shelter. But some owners may not know how to care for them. The owners may feed them the wrong food. In some cases, the owner might mistreat the animals. Owners may get tired of their pets. Sometimes, they leave them out on the streets. Some homeless animals don't know how to find food on their own. So they go hungry.

Wild animals are different. They have always lived in nature. They know how to find their own food and shelter. But in today's world, this isn't always easy. While building our cities, people have destroyed many animal **habitats**. Hunters have killed many wild animals. And people sometimes pollute water and food supplies. This has **endangered** many animals. Others have become **extinct**.

Abandoned cats may be forced to search for food in trash cans.

a bald eagle in its nest

Scientists estimate that 22 percent of all species will be extinct by the year 2022 if we don't do something to save these animals.

Sheep depend on their owners for food and shelter.

Giving Shelter

SPCA stands for the Society for the Prevention of Cruelty to Animals. This organization works for the safety and health of animals around the United States. Meet Alice Shanahan, a director at an SPCA office in New York.

Jessica: How can kids help the SPCA protect animals?

Alice: Many schools have formed pet clubs. [They] do projects to benefit shelter animals. School and scout groups visit shelters on a regular basis. They often bake dog biscuits or make cat toys and sell them [to raise money for us].

Jessica: What about working with the animals?

Alice: Kids help by offering **TLC** to all the pups. [They] help with cleaning and feeding.

Jessica: Why is this important?

Alice: The work is very important both for the kids and for the shelter. [The kids] are learning to give something back to the animals and to their community. [The] animals [are helped by their fund-raising] and their companionship. And the flyers they make help our animals find homes.

Homemade Dog Biscuits

You can sell biscuits to raise money for your local shelter. Just follow the steps in this easy recipe. These bites are truly bark-worthy!

 Preheat the oven to 350°F. Mix the flour and oats together.

Ingredients

2 cups of whole-wheat flour

1 cup of rolled oats

$\frac{1}{3}$ cup of peanut butter

$1\frac{1}{4}$ cups of hot water

 Mix in the peanut butter and hot water. If the mixture is too sticky, you may want to add more flour.

 Knead the dough and roll it out (about $\frac{1}{4}$ inch thick).

4 Use a dog-bone cookie cutter to cut the dough into several pieces.

5 Lightly grease a cookie sheet and bake the biscuits for 40 minutes at 350°F. Let them cool overnight.

For the Birds

As the world changes, wild animals must find new ways to survive. Humans can help. In 2011, millions of gallons of oil spilled off the coast of New Zealand. The oil coated the feathers of penguins in the water. As the birds tried to clean off the oil, they ingested it and became sick. The special feathers that usually kept them warm were damaged. Each penguin had to be cleaned by hand.

A call for help went out to the world. People began to knit sweaters for the birds. They kept the penguins warm while waiting for their bath. And they also prevented the birds from swallowing the oil.

Many rescue projects need hands-on help. Local shelters need people who will play with animals waiting to be **adopted**. Even young children can help with that.

A rescued penguin wears a sweater to stay warm after an oil spill.

A Flood of Volunteers

When Hurricane Katrina hit the Gulf Coast in 2005, dirty water flooded New Orleans. About 250,000 pets were without homes. Some pets were found on roofs. Others were trapped inside. Volunteers came together for one of the largest animal rescues in history.

a dog stranded on a ruined home in New Orleans

Volunteers clean a gull after an oil spill in the Gulf of Mexico.

Paw Protection

Animal **abuse** is a terrible problem. Each year, thousands of animals are beaten. Dogs are forced to fight and kill other dogs. The most common forms of abuse are **neglect** and **abandonment**. The animals simply are not cared for properly.

Signs of neglect include wounds and other skin problems. The animal may seem confused, very sleepy, or walk as if hurt. These may be signs that the owner needs help. Or it may mean that the animals need rescuing. If you see an animal like this, report it to the SPCA.

Dogs are the most commonly abused animals in America. This one was rescued from a ring of dog fighters.

A Brave Tail

Kindness, not abuse, is the best way to train animals. Faith was a dog born with three legs. There were two in back and one in front. The front one never grew and had to be cut off. Her guardians taught her to walk on two legs. They used peanut butter to reward her.

By the Numbers

Dinosaurs lived long ago. But now, all that's left behind are their giant bones. Sadly, some species die out. They become extinct for many reasons. Sometimes, animals can't find food. Then, they can't survive. Other species are hunted to extinction.

The Endangered Species Act was passed by the United States Congress in 1973. It protects endangered animals and plants. It also protects living things that are **threatened**. These are species that are close to being endangered. Lots of people are working hard to make sure these animals are protected. But they need more help.

Across the world, one out of eight birds is endangered.

Monkey Business

There are more than 250 species of monkeys. Half are threatened. Some are hunted for their meat in Africa. Concerned people have found ways to raise these monkeys in protected areas. They hope this will save these rare creatures.

a rare proboscis monkey

Helping the Hunted

Some animals are endangered. Yet people still buy products that are made from them. Writing to officials is one way to stop this. Agreements between governments can make it harder to hunt animals.

a golden lion tamarin with her baby

DIG DEEPER!

Keeping Count

Animals around the world need our help. The ones here may need it most of all. Their numbers are critically low. But with time, money, and steady voices, we may be able to save these endangered species. Look below to see how many are left.

25–35
Amur Leopard
Far East Russia and North East China

40–60
Javan Rhinoceros
Indonesia

1,600
Giant
Panda
China

720
Mountain Gorilla
Africa

500
Philippine Eagle
Philippines

In Our Hands

Animals make our world better in so many ways. Now they need our help. They face abuse. Some are endangered. Life is becoming harder for many creatures. But animals don't have a voice. Instead, we must raise our voices together to speak for them.

There are many animal rights groups that speak out against people who mistreat animals. These **activists** want laws that will protect animals. Many animal rights activists won't buy or wear fur coats. Some don't eat animals. Many activists argue against animals being used for science experiments. They believe these practices make animals suffer. Activists say we are not showing respect for animals and their lives.

There are many groups that help protect wildlife. The World Wildlife Fund (WWF) works in the poorest countries. It prevents **poaching**. The group helps countries join together to patrol forests. The patrols protect the wildlife from being stolen or killed by the poachers. Some have saved baby animals from being stolen and sold to circuses or zoos. The WWF also helps protect animal habitats from **pollution**.

PROTECT TIGERS

Students come together to ask officials to protect tigers.

Activists work to protect animals from painful experiments.

Without your voice the torture will continue

Animals in Labs Need Your Help

In Defense of Animals •

"The greatness of a nation and its moral progress can be judged by the way its animals are treated."
—Mohandas Gandhi

Place Savers

The **conservation** movement began over 40 years ago. It was started to prevent the killing of the rarest animals. Now, activists watch over the places where these animals live, too. Areas where rare animals build their homes and hunt are protected by new laws. You can support a conservation group by giving money or time.

In an Uproar

Lions and other big cats are now rare in the wild. Conservation workers are trying to open up the land between nature preserves in Africa. This would allow lions to more easily mate and have families.

The year 2022 is the Year of the Tiger in China. Some people hope to double the number of tigers in the wild by then.

To more than **DOUBLE** TIGER population (6,400 in 2022)

Money in the Bank

When times are hard, people have trouble feeding their families. Sometimes, they also need food for their pets, too. One way to help is to give food to an animal food bank. You can collect food or raise money to buy it.

Giving money is another way to help. Some people raise money to help wild animals. Others send money to farms or zoos. Some programs focus on one kind of animal, such as whales. You can also "adopt" a wild animal of your own. You can help to pay for its food or home. It's a special way to connect with animals.

collecting dog food

Smart Shopping

Even if you don't give money to an animal **charity**, you can use your money to help animals. When you buy something, look for the Leaping Bunny logo. That means no animals were hurt making it.

More Ways to Help

Food banks collect donations of dog and cat food. But there are many other items they accept to help out families in need. Here are a few:

- flea medicine
- cat and dog toys
- pet beds
- kitty litter

The arctic fox is protected by the World Wildlife Fund.

33

DIG DEEPER!

Friends of a Feather

There are lots of ways to **donate** time or money to help animals. It's most fun when you organize your friends and work together. Check out the ideas below, and try your favorite one.

Dog Walk

Map out a short route around your neighborhood. Post flyers about your event two weeks in advance. Allow people to enter the event by donating animal food, treats, beds, and toys. The first dog to complete the walk will win a portion of the donations. The remaining entry fees can be donated to a local animal shelter.

Best in Show

Why not raise money for animals by working with man's best friend? Organize a dog show with your neighbors. Invite your neighbors to enter their dogs in the contest for a fee. Award simple prizes for furriest dog, tallest dog, and best tail wagging. Donate the money you make to your local shelter.

School's Funniest Pet

Invite classmates to enter a contest for the school's funniest pet. Students can submit videos of their pet from home or class. The video should show how funny the pet is. To enter, students donate animal food, treats, beds, and toys. Look through the videos carefully and select the top 10. Then, allow students to vote for the funniest video. Donate the animal items to an organization.

Citizen Scientists

Another way to help animals is to study them. Scientists watch to see how animals behave. They study what animals need to survive. Young scientists can count animals. It's simple to do. And it can show if there are changes over time. Scientists also report new animals in the area or any strange behaviors. The more we know about animals, the more we can find ways to help them.

Project Noah

Scientists around the world are working together to study animals. You can help by taking a picture of the animals in your neighborhood. Then, share what you find with other nature lovers online. Scientists use the photos to observe and compare animals from around the world. Log onto *ProjectNoah.org* to find out more.

Lost Ladybugs

Across the country, some types of ladybugs are disappearing. Scientists don't know why it's happening, but they want to learn more. Whenever you find a ladybug, take a picture. Then, upload it to *LostLadybug.org*. If you can't find any ladybugs, let them know that, too. It's useful for scientists to know where the ladybugs are found, as well as where they are not found.

Caring Careers

There are many ways to help animals. One of the best ways is to go to school and train for a career in caring for animals. Most of these careers require biology and **zoology** classes in college. The following careers are just some of the ways you can help.

Veterinarians are animal doctors. Some vets are experts at helping pets and domestic animals. Other vets specialize in wild animals.

Park rangers care for our nation's wild areas. They make sure animals are safe and help protect the environment for animals.

Wildlife rehabilitators take care of injured animals for a short time. When the animal is ready, they help it adjust to life in the wild.

STOP! THINK...

- Which job sounds the most interesting to you?

- Which career do you think is the best way to help animals?

- If you're interested in one of these careers, what are some steps you can take to find out more?

Animal trainers teach animals how to behave and obey commands.

Raise Your Voice

Animals can't speak for themselves. So we must speak for them. People must take action. There are many ways you can help, from raising money for a shelter to keeping our planet safe for animals. Everything makes a difference. If we work together, these amazing creatures will share our world for years to come.

"Let's do the work that needs to be done, with love and compassion."
—Jane Goodall

Glossary

abandonment—the state of being left behind

abuse—to hurt or harm

activists—people who act to bring about change, especially political change

adopted—taken on as someone's responsibility

animal trainers—people who train animals to act in specific ways and obey commands

biologists—people who study biology, an area of science that deals with living things

captivity—being contained in an area, not being able to leave

charity—a group set up to provide help and money to a certain cause

companion—one who acts as a friend and serves another

conservation—the protection of something such as the environment

domesticated—adapted to life with humans

donate—to give without compensation

ecosystem—the community of living things in a specific place

endangered—in danger of disappearing from Earth

environment—a set of complete factors that form an ecosystem that includes soil, climate, and living things

expressions—ways in which the face appears to show feelings

extinct—no longer existing in the world

fertilizer—solid waste from farm animals that is added to soil to help plants grow

gestures—movements of the body (usually arms or hands) that show ideas or feelings

habitats—the places where living things belong naturally

neglect—to give little attention to

park rangers—people who are in charge of caring for wild areas of land

poaching—stealing or killing animals illegally

pollution—the act or process of making land, water, and air dirty or unsafe for use

service animals—animals trained to help people that have a physical or mental limitation

species—a class of living things with similar features

threatened—close to being endangered

TLC—tender loving care

veterinarians—people who are doctors to animals

volunteer—someone who does a job willingly without being paid

wildlife rehabilitators—people who help injured or sick animals heal so they can return to the wild

working animals—trained animals that perform work that is difficult for humans to perform

zoology—an area of biology that focuses on animals

Index

Bibliography

BishopRoby, Joshua. *The World of Animals.* Teacher Created Materials, 2008.

Learn how scientists classify animals and what makes animals different from humans.

Hoare, Ben. *Eyewitness: Endangered Animals.* DK Children, 2010.

Look at creatures around the world that are currently threatened with extinction and the many ways we can help them survive.

Lessem, Don. *Dinosaurs to Dodos: An Encyclopedia of Extinct Animals.* Scholastic, 1999.

Research extinct animals, what led to their extinction, and the modern scientific discoveries that reveal their lost worlds.

Palika, Liz and Miller, Katherine A. *Animals at Work (ASPCA Kids).* Howell Book House, 2009.

Discover how dogs protect livestock, guide people, pull sleds and wagons, and more. Also read about horses who serve in the military and law enforcement and cats who provide therapy to the sick and elderly.

Steiger, Brad and Steiger, Sherry Hansen. *The Mysteries of Animal Intelligence: True Stories of Animals with Amazing Abilities.* Tor Books, 2007.

These stories reveal the intelligence, bravery, and skills of different kinds of animals and how they have helped humans.

More to Explore

Association of Zoos & Aquariums
http://www.aza.org
> Here you can find ways that kids and families can become more educated and involved with wildlife conservation.

Delta Society: Pet Partners
http://www.deltasociety.org
> Learn how pet therapy works. Find training in your area if you are interested in getting your pet involved.

Kids' Planet
http://www.kidsplanet.org
> This website includes many interactive features, such as games, a world map, electronic fact sheets on over 50 species, information on wolves, and more cool stuff.

National Wildlife Federation
http://www.nwf.org
> This site presents various wildlife preservation causes. There is even a tab at the top just for kids.

World Wildlife Fund
http://www.worldwildlife.org
> Find out about different endangered species and what is being done to protect them. Under *What We Do*, click *Protect Species*. Also, you can see what you, personally, can do to help. Under *How To Help* click *Make It Personal*.

About the Author

Jessica Cohn grew up in Michigan, where she volunteered in school and the Girl Scouts. She has a bachelor's degree in English and a master's in written communications. She has worked in educational publishing for more than a decade as a writer and an editor. She has written articles and books on many subjects, including animals. She is married and has two sons. The family is based in New York state, where they are friends to all animals.